ASOGWA JOY LOVE

Ablaze After the Waters

Copyright © 2025 by Asogwa Joy Love

All rights reserved. No part of this publication may be reproduced, stored or transmitted in any form or by any means, electronic, mechanical, photocopying, recording, scanning, or otherwise without written permission from the publisher. It is illegal to copy this book, post it to a website, or distribute it by any other means without permission.

Asogwa Joy Love asserts the moral right to be identified as the author of this work.

Asogwa Joy Love has no responsibility for the persistence or accuracy of URLs for external or third-party Internet Websites referred to in this publication and does not guarantee that any content on such Websites is, or will remain, accurate or appropriate.

First edition

This book was professionally typeset on Reedsy.
Find out more at reedsy.com

Contents

1. The Omen in the River — 1
2. The Whispering Current — 4
3. Vanishing Waters — 8
4. Shadows Beneath the Surface — 11
5. The Drowning Voices — 15
6. The Vanishing Line — 18
7. The Unseen Baptism — 21
8. Beneath the Surface — 25
9. The Drowned Shall Rise — 28
10. The Water Remembers — 31
11. The Whispering Font — 35
12. Drenched in Shadows — 39

1

The Omen in the River

The river ran smooth and dark beneath the waning light of dusk. Elias Foster stood at the edge of the gathered crowd, his notepad gripped tightly in one hand, the other resting in his jacket pocket where his recorder was hidden. He had come to observe, to document, to dissect this strange ritual that, according to local rumors, held far more power than it should.

A row of lanterns flickered along the banks, their glow stretching across the water like ghostly fingers. The congregation, clothed in white robes, stood in silent anticipation, eyes fixed on the woman stepping forward. She was young, perhaps in her mid-twenties, her face pale but resolute as she descended into the river.

Reverend Malcolm stood waist-deep in the water, his hands outstretched. His voice, rich and steady, carried across the hush of the night. "We come before God, seeking renewal. We bury the old self and rise anew."

Elias scribbled down the words, his journalist's mind already framing the opening of his article. Another small-town spectacle, another story of blind faith wrapped in myth. He had seen dozens of these ceremonies, though none quite as secretive as this one. The invitation had been whispered, not printed. The location had changed twice before tonight. Why?

The woman in the water clasped her hands together, whispering words Elias couldn't catch. Then, with reverence, the reverend placed a firm hand on the crown of her head and another on her back.

"In the name of the Father, the Son, and the Holy Spirit, you are baptized."

He pressed her down beneath the water.

A gasp rippled through the crowd.

Elias leaned forward, frowning. He could see it too—the water, crystal clear only moments ago, now darkened, as though something beneath the surface was bleeding into it.

The reverend hesitated, his lips parting in surprise. Then, just as quickly, he pulled the woman back up.

She came up choking, gasping for breath. Her hands clawed at the air before gripping the reverend's arms. Her eyes—Elias swore he saw something shift in them. A flicker of light? A shadow?

A murmur spread through the onlookers. The woman clutched her chest, trembling. The river at her feet was still stained red. Not the wild red of blood, but something subtler, darker—like ink spreading through parchment.

The reverend quickly regained his composure. "Rejoice!" he declared. "For she has been reborn."

The congregation clapped hesitantly, but the energy had changed. There was an unease, a tension that curled around the air like mist.

Elias felt his pulse quicken. He turned his attention to the river. The stain was dissipating, vanishing as though it had never been there.

He barely noticed the woman stepping back onto the shore, still shaking, eyes unfocused. She whispered something to herself, over and over. Elias strained to hear.

"The fire... the fire... the fire..."

The reverend placed a hand on her shoulder and led her toward the others, murmuring reassurances.

Elias exhaled, glancing down at his notes. His handwriting was uneven, rushed. He had documented revivals before, had seen people collapse in fervor, in supposed divine ecstasy. But this—this was different.

The woman didn't look overjoyed. She looked terrified.

As the crowd began to disperse, Elias tucked his notepad away. He took a step closer to the river's edge, watching the water flow past in gentle ripples. He crouched, dipping his fingers into the current. It felt normal. Cool. Harmless. But something about it still made his skin crawl.

A hand gripped his shoulder.

He spun, heart hammering.

It was the reverend.

"You shouldn't linger," Malcolm said quietly. His eyes held something knowing, something guarded. "Not tonight."

Elias straightened. "What happened back there?"

The reverend smiled—a tight, polite thing. "A baptism."

Before Elias could press further, the reverend turned and walked away, his robe flowing behind him.

Elias exhaled sharply, glancing back at the river one last time. Then he turned to leave, his mind already racing with questions.

By morning, the woman would be gone.

2

The Whispering Current

The town of Black Hollow was the kind of place that felt frozen in time. Its streets, lined with aging brick buildings and dimly lit storefronts, bore the weight of secrets buried beneath decades of whispers. Elias had arrived two days ago, expecting nothing more than a strange but ultimately explainable religious gathering. But after what he had witnessed at the river, something gnawed at him—something he couldn't shake.

Now, in the early morning light, he found himself walking back toward the riverbank. The dirt path was still damp from the night before, the air thick with the scent of earth and something faintly metallic. He had barely slept, his mind looping over the image of the woman rising from the water—her trembling hands, her unfocused gaze, the cryptic words that had spilled from her lips.

The fire.

He pulled out his notepad, flipping through the hastily scrawled notes from the night before. Had she seen something beneath the surface? Felt something? And the water—he hadn't imagined that. It had darkened, changed, if only for a moment.

Reaching the river's edge, he crouched, dipping his hand into the water again. Cool, just like last night. Normal. But something about it still made him uneasy.

A rustling from the tree line made him stiffen. He turned sharply, scanning the woods. Nothing.

Then—another sound.

A whisper.

Low. Indistinct.

He held his breath, listening. It was faint, threading through the air like a breath of wind, but it was there. The words were unintelligible, more sensation than sound, as if the river itself was murmuring beneath the steady current.

Elias stood abruptly, his pulse quickening. He was alone. There was no one in sight, no movement beyond the lazy swaying of branches in the morning breeze.

He took a step back from the water. The whispering had stopped.

With a deep breath, he forced himself to focus. He needed to find the woman from last night. She had to still be in town. Someone had to know who she was.

The Black Hollow General Store sat on the corner of Main Street, its wooden sign creaking in protest against the wind. Inside, the place smelled of dust and aged wood, the shelves lined with canned goods, faded postcards, and an odd collection of religious trinkets.

An older woman stood behind the counter, her sharp blue eyes tracking him the moment he entered.

"Morning," Elias said, offering a polite nod.

She didn't return the greeting. "You're the reporter," she said instead.

It wasn't a question.

Elias hesitated before stepping forward. "Word travels fast."

"In a town this size, word never stops traveling." She wiped her hands on her apron and leaned against the counter. "You were at the river last night."

Elias studied her, considering his next words. "Yes. I was."

The woman pursed her lips, then glanced toward the front window, as if checking to see if anyone was watching. After a moment, she sighed and lowered her voice.

"You should leave this alone."

Elias felt a prickle of irritation. "Why?"

"Because nothing good comes from digging too deep." She held his gaze, her expression unreadable. "Especially not here."

Elias leaned on the counter. "The woman who was baptized—who is she?"

The old woman hesitated. Then, after a moment, she muttered, "Her name's Claire Mathis."

Finally, a lead. He scribbled the name down. "Where can I find her?"

"That's the thing," the woman said, voice quieter now. "You can't."

Elias frowned. "What do you mean?"

She exhaled through her nose, folding her arms. "She left town early this morning. Her parents said she packed a bag and took off before sunrise. No warning. Just gone."

Elias felt a slow chill creep over him.

Gone?

He thought of the way she had looked after the baptism—shaken, muttering about fire. Had she seen something? Had something frightened her enough to make her run?

Or had someone told her to?

The old woman studied him for a long moment before speaking again, softer this time.

"She's not the first."

Elias stiffened. "What do you mean?"

The woman's gaze flickered toward the door again, as if deciding whether she should continue. Then, finally, she spoke.

"There have been others. Baptized in that river. And afterward... they leave. Always. Some within days, some within hours. They don't say goodbye. They don't come back."

A heavy silence settled between them.

Elias tightened his grip on his pen. "Where do they go?"

The woman shook her head. "No one knows. They don't just leave town.

They disappear."

Elias felt his pulse quicken. The weight of the river, the whispers in the trees, the way the water had darkened—he had brushed it off as illusion, as the mind playing tricks in the dark.

But now?

Now, he wasn't so sure.

3

Vanishing Waters

Elias sat in his motel room, the dim glow of his laptop screen casting long shadows across the walls. The room smelled of stale air and old fabric, but he barely noticed. His fingers hovered over the keyboard, his mind racing with everything he had learned that morning.

Claire Mathis had left town without a trace. Not a word to her friends, not a goodbye to her family—just gone, like the others before her.

He leaned back, rubbing a hand over his face. It didn't add up. He had covered religious revivals, exorcisms, faith healings—but this? This was different. People didn't just vanish after a baptism.

His eyes flickered to the recorder sitting on the nightstand. He replayed the recording from last night, his own voice murmuring notes into the speaker:

"Baptism. River darkened. Claire seemed... altered. Mentioned fire. Reverend Malcolm's reaction—controlled, but uneasy."

He paused the recording, rewinding it a few seconds. There—just after Claire had risen from the water, barely audible beneath the murmurs of the crowd.

A whisper.

Not from Claire. Not from the reverend. It was something else. A voice, low and almost inhuman, buried beneath the noise.

Elias sat up straighter. He adjusted the volume, listening again.

It wasn't just one whisper. There were many.

He swallowed, his pulse thudding in his ears. He had stood right there, near the riverbank, and heard nothing unusual in the moment. But the recording had caught something he hadn't.

He grabbed his jacket, shoved the recorder into his pocket, and headed for the door.

The river looked different in the daylight. The lanterns and shadows of the night before had masked its full breadth, but now, under the harsh afternoon sun, the water stretched wide and unassuming.

Elias stood at the same spot where Claire had been baptized, staring at the current. It moved slow, calm. Too calm.

A shiver crawled up his spine.

He crouched down and reached out, dipping his fingers into the water. The cool sensation was immediate, sending a small jolt through his arm. He pulled his hand back and stared at the droplets clinging to his skin.

Something about it felt... wrong.

Not cold. Not warm. Just... empty.

He clenched his fingers, then wiped his hand on his jeans before standing.

A sound carried through the trees. A rustling.

He turned sharply.

Nothing.

And then—movement. A figure in the distance, half-hidden behind a thick oak tree.

Elias' breath caught. "Hey!"

The figure didn't move.

He took a cautious step forward. "Who's there?"

Silence.

His heart pounded as he advanced. The figure was draped in what looked like a robe—white, like the ones worn during the baptisms. But as he drew closer, the details sharpened.

The robe wasn't white. It was pale, sun-bleached, worn thin by time. The fabric clung to the shape beneath it, the hood shadowing the face.

Elias swallowed hard.

Something about the figure's posture was unnatural. Stiff. Motionless.

A gust of wind rustled the leaves, but the figure didn't react.

Elias took another step. "Did you know Claire Mathis?"

No answer.

He hesitated, then glanced down. The ground beneath the figure was damp. A small puddle formed around its feet, as if water was seeping from the robe itself.

His chest tightened.

The figure lifted its head—just slightly. Enough for him to see the outline of a chin, the suggestion of lips.

But no eyes.

Elias stumbled back, his breath coming short.

The figure took a step forward.

Elias turned and bolted.

He sprinted toward the road, his feet pounding against the dirt, lungs burning as he gasped for air. He didn't dare look back, didn't want to see if the thing was following him.

Only when he reached the edge of town did he stop, doubling over, hands on his knees. His whole body trembled, his mind struggling to process what he had seen.

No. Not seen.

Imagined.

It had to be his mind playing tricks on him. The tension, the mystery—it was getting to him.

He forced himself to take deep, steadying breaths.

But when he glanced down at his jeans, his stomach clenched.

Water.

Dark, ink-stained droplets soaked into the fabric.

And he hadn't touched the river.

4

Shadows Beneath the Surface

Elias sat in his motel room, staring at the damp stain on his jeans. The water had dried now, but a faint discoloration remained, like a bruise on fabric. He had wiped his hands, checked his shoes—nothing. There was no logical way he should have been wet. And yet, the water had been there, clinging to him.

His fingers hovered over the keyboard of his laptop, but the words refused to come. He had spent years chasing stories—political scandals, urban legends, supernatural hoaxes. But this? This was different. The weight of it settled in his chest like a stone.

A knock at the door jolted him upright.

He hesitated before moving, the echo of his own footsteps sounding too loud in the quiet room. When he cracked the door open, the woman from the general store stood in the dimly lit hallway, a cigarette trembling between her fingers.

"We need to talk."

Elias stepped aside, letting her in. She didn't sit. Instead, she paced near the window, exhaling smoke into the stale air.

"You went back to the river, didn't you?" she asked, her voice edged with something that could have been fear.

Elias folded his arms. "What do you know about that place?"

She sighed, flicking ash onto the carpet. "More than I'd like to."

Elias narrowed his eyes. "Tell me about the others. The ones who disappeared after baptism."

She was quiet for a long moment, then turned to face him. "The first one was over forty years ago. A boy named Matthew Grayson. I was just a kid, but I remember his parents—how they searched for him, how they never found him. Then, a few years later, another one. A girl. Same story. It kept happening, always after baptism, always without warning."

Elias' mind raced. "And no one reported it? No police investigations?"

A bitter laugh escaped her lips. "You don't understand this town, Mr. Finch. Some things just don't get reported."

Elias felt a prickle of unease. "Why not?"

She flicked the cigarette into the sink and turned to him, her voice barely above a whisper.

"Because they weren't missing."

Elias frowned. "What do you mean?"

"They weren't gone. Not in the way you think."

She took a step closer. "Some people have seen them. Not as they were, but... changed. Standing near the river, watching. Silent."

Elias' breath caught. He thought of the figure in the woods, the dripping robe, the absence of eyes.

"You saw one, didn't you?" she asked.

He clenched his jaw. "I don't know what I saw."

She gave him a knowing look. "You should leave, Mr. Finch."

Elias exhaled sharply, running a hand through his hair. "Not yet."

The woman shook her head. "You think this is just a story. A mystery to solve. But you don't understand—this thing, whatever it is, it doesn't want to be understood. And the more you dig, the more it sees you."

A chill ran through him.

The woman turned to leave, then hesitated at the door. "Do yourself a favor. When the sun sets, don't go near the water."

And with that, she was gone.

SHADOWS BENEATH THE SURFACE

Elias tried to sleep, but his mind wouldn't let him.

Every time he closed his eyes, he saw the river. The way the water had darkened around Claire, the way the whispers had bled into the night.

And the figure.

He needed answers.

Grabbing his keys and recorder, he stepped outside into the cool night air. The streets were empty, the town swallowed by an unsettling silence.

It took him twenty minutes to reach the river.

The water gleamed under the moonlight, deceptively still. He crouched near the edge, pressing record on his device.

"This is Elias Finch. I'm at Black Hollow River, 11:37 p.m. No sign of activity."

The wind rustled the trees.

Then—something else.

A soft ripple, as if something had just slipped beneath the surface.

Elias stiffened. He aimed his flashlight at the water, the beam cutting through the darkness. The river appeared empty. But then—movement. A shadow, deep beneath the current, shifting.

His pulse pounded. He leaned in closer.

A whisper drifted through the air.

This time, it wasn't coming from behind him.

It was coming from the water.

The whisper grew louder, words still indistinct but urgent, insistent. Elias' breath hitched as a shape began to rise beneath the surface—pale, blurred, reaching.

A hand.

A human hand.

But as it broke the surface, water dripping from fingers that looked impossibly long, impossibly thin, Elias stumbled back, his flashlight shaking in his grip.

The hand did not belong to Claire.

And it was not alone.

More shapes stirred beneath the water, whispering, rising.
Elias turned and ran.

5

The Drowning Voices

Elias ran without looking back, the whispers from the river following him like a phantom chorus. His lungs burned, his legs ached, but he didn't dare stop—not until he was safely back in town. Even then, the sound seemed to linger in his ears, pressing against his thoughts like damp fingers.

By the time he reached his motel room, his hands were shaking. He fumbled with the key, cursing under his breath, before finally shoving the door open and locking it behind him. The silence inside was deafening.

He sank into the chair by the window, staring at the recorder still clutched in his fingers. Slowly, he rewound the tape and pressed play.

At first, there was nothing but the sound of his own breathing, then the rustling of the wind through the trees.

And then, the whispering began.

Elias felt his stomach tighten. The voices weren't singular. They layered over one another, rising and falling, their words slipping in and out of coherence. He strained to make them out.

"He comes."

"The water remembers."

"Join us."

Elias swallowed hard, his pulse hammering in his throat. He hit stop, unable to listen any further.

A knock at the door made him nearly jump out of his chair.

His heart pounded as he stood and hesitated before reaching for the doorknob. The motel had been empty when he arrived—he hadn't seen another guest, hadn't heard a single car pull into the lot. Who the hell would be knocking at this hour?

He pressed his ear against the wood.

Silence.

Another knock—this time slower, deliberate.

Elias' fingers hovered over the lock.

"Who is it?" His voice was hoarse.

No answer.

He backed away. His mind raced through possibilities—was it the woman from earlier? Had she changed her mind about warning him?

Or was it someone else?

He swallowed hard, then grabbed the recorder and turned it back on. If something was about to happen, he wanted proof.

A deep breath. Then, he unlocked the door and pulled it open.

Nothing.

The hallway was empty.

A cold draft coiled around him, and he shuddered. His instincts screamed at him to shut the door, but his eyes drifted downward.

The motel's thin, brown carpet was damp. A trail of wet footprints led from his doorway back down the hall.

Bare footprints.

His breath hitched. They were fresh, glistening under the dim light. And they led to nowhere—stopping abruptly just a few feet away, as if whoever had been standing there had simply ceased to exist.

Elias took a step back into his room and slammed the door shut, bolting it this time.

He pressed his back against the wall, trying to steady his breathing. He had seen strange things before, but this—this was different. This wasn't some hoax or urban legend. It was real.

And it was getting closer.

He forced himself to think. He needed answers. The woman from the store had known something. The reverend had looked uneasy after Claire's baptism. Someone in this town knew what was happening, and he had no intention of leaving until he found out.

Pulling his notebook from his bag, he scribbled down a list:
1. Claire's family – What do they know?
2. Reverend Malcolm – What is he hiding?
3. The woman from the store – Find her again.
4. The river – Why does the water change?

His pen hesitated over the last point.

1. The voices – What are they?

Elias exhaled sharply, shutting the notebook. He had spent years chasing stories that never amounted to anything. But this time, the story was chasing him.

And he wasn't sure if he wanted to be caught.

6

The Vanishing Line

Elias barely slept. The motel room, once just another forgettable stop in his journey, now felt like a cage. The whispering hadn't stopped. It had burrowed into his mind, lurking just beneath the surface of his thoughts, waiting for silence to seep through the cracks.

At some point, exhaustion took over, and he drifted into a restless slumber. But even in sleep, there was no escape.

He was at the river again.

The moon hung low, swollen and pale, casting its sickly glow over the water. The current was still, but the darkness beneath the surface churned. A figure stood at the edge—a girl in a white dress, her hair hanging in wet tangles over her face.

Claire.

She turned slowly, her arms hanging limp at her sides. Her eyes—if they were eyes—were hollow, filled with nothing but the blackness of the river. She opened her mouth, and water spilled out, gushing in torrents as if she were drowning from the inside.

"Help me," she choked.

Then, something reached up from the depths, skeletal fingers curling around her ankle.

She didn't scream. She didn't fight.

She only whispered, *"You're next."*

The river swallowed her whole.

Elias woke with a violent gasp, his heart hammering against his ribs. His skin was slick with sweat, and for one disorienting moment, he thought he could still hear the water dripping.

Then, the knocking started.

Slow. Rhythmic.

He forced himself to move, his limbs feeling like lead. He reached for the recorder on the nightstand, his fingers trembling as he pressed the button.

"This is Elias Finch. Motel room 14. It's 4:12 a.m. Someone is at my door."

The knocking came again.

He crept toward the peephole, his breath held tight in his chest. The hallway was empty.

A shiver crawled up his spine.

Another knock—so close this time, as if it came from the other side of the door rather than outside it.

He gritted his teeth and yanked the door open.

Nothing.

The corridor stretched before him, eerily still. The flickering light overhead buzzed faintly, casting long, shifting shadows.

He stepped out cautiously, glancing in both directions. The motel office was dark, the entire building dead quiet. A damp chill settled in the air, and he instinctively looked down.

Wet footprints.

Bare feet. Leading away from his door.

His pulse thundered in his ears. He followed them, each step slower than the last. They led to the stairs, then out into the gravel parking lot. The early morning air was thick with fog, swirling in slow tendrils across the ground.

The footprints didn't stop at the lot. They continued toward the road. Toward the river.

Elias hesitated. Every rational part of him screamed to turn back.

Instead, he pressed record again.

"I'm following something," he whispered. "I don't know who... or what. But I have to know."

The town was lifeless at this hour. No cars. No voices. Just the rhythmic sound of his own footsteps on the pavement.

As he neared the river, the mist grew denser, clinging to the trees like a living thing. The footprints became harder to see, fading as if the earth itself had swallowed them.

Then, the whispering returned.

Not behind him.

Not around him.

But in front of him.

He froze, his breath hitching. The river was only a few yards away, its surface glassy and unmoving.

A figure stood at the edge.

Elias' throat went dry. It wasn't Claire. This was something else—taller, leaner, draped in what looked like the remnants of a baptismal robe. Its arms hung stiffly at its sides, its head tilted at an unnatural angle.

Then, it took a step forward, its bare feet pressing into the damp earth.

Elias staggered back.

His mind screamed at him to run, but his body refused to obey.

The figure lifted an arm—slowly, almost mechanically.

Pointing.

At him.

A low, distorted voice slithered through the air.

"You shouldn't be here."

Elias stumbled, his hands shaking so violently that he nearly dropped the recorder. He turned on his heel and ran, not stopping until the motel was in sight.

He didn't look back.

Not even when the whisper followed him all the way back.

7

The Unseen Baptism

Elias locked the motel room door behind him, his chest heaving with ragged breaths. He pressed his back against the wooden surface, squeezing his eyes shut as he tried to push out the image of the figure by the river—the thing that had whispered to him.

His hands trembled as he reached for his recorder. He pressed play, expecting to hear his own frantic footsteps or the pounding of his heart. But what came through the tiny speaker sent an icy shiver through his spine.

It wasn't just his footsteps.

There was something else.

A second set of footsteps—soft, deliberate, following him.

Elias' blood ran cold. He rewound the tape and played it again, straining to hear beyond the rustling wind.

Step. Step. Whisper.

"He walks where he shouldn't."

He yanked the batteries out of the recorder, tossing it onto the bed like it had burned him. He needed to get out of here. He needed answers.

Claire's parents. They had been at the baptism. They had seen something.

He grabbed his jacket and forced himself to step outside. The early morning fog still clung to the air, thick and unyielding. The town felt different now—too quiet, as if it were waiting for something.

Elias kept his pace steady as he walked toward the house he had seen the family enter after the baptism. He knocked once. Then twice.

No answer.

He tried again, this time harder.

A soft creak. The door opened an inch.

A woman's bloodshot eyes peeked through the gap. It was Claire's mother, but she looked different—her face gaunt, her lips cracked, her skin pale as if she hadn't slept in days.

Elias took a cautious step forward. "Mrs. Harding?"

The woman flinched at her own name. Her gaze darted behind Elias, scanning the street as though she expected something—or someone—to be there.

"You shouldn't be here," she whispered, echoing the words from the river.

Elias felt his stomach twist. "I need to talk to you about what happened at the baptism."

The woman's breath hitched. "No. No, you don't."

"Please," he pressed. "Something is happening. I—" He hesitated before lowering his voice. "I saw Claire at the river."

Mrs. Harding went rigid.

A sharp intake of breath.

Her grip on the door tightened.

"You're lying," she whispered.

"I'm not," Elias said carefully. "I saw her. She—she wasn't herself."

The woman's body shook. "Because it's not her."

Elias' heart pounded. "Then what is it?"

For a long moment, the woman said nothing. Then, slowly, she unlatched the door and stepped aside.

Inside, the house felt heavy, as if the very walls were soaked with sorrow. The air carried the faint scent of damp wood and something else—something metallic, like rust.

Mrs. Harding led him to the living room. There were no family photos, no signs of warmth. Just drawn curtains and a single candle flickering on the coffee table.

"You shouldn't have come," she said, her voice hollow. "You've seen it now. It knows you see it."

Elias sat forward. "What is it?"

The woman's fingers curled into the fabric of her dress. "It comes for them."

"Who?"

She swallowed hard. "The ones who enter the water."

Elias' pulse quickened. "The baptized?"

Mrs. Harding nodded. Her hands trembled as she picked up the candle, staring into the flame as if seeking answers within it. "Not all of them," she said. "Just some. The ones it chooses."

Elias felt his throat go dry. "Claire?"

Tears welled in the woman's eyes. "She never came back from the river," she whispered. "Not really. What we brought home that night… wasn't her."

A chill settled deep in Elias' bones. "Then what was it?"

Mrs. Harding's lips quivered. "Something old. Something hungry."

The room seemed to darken as the candle flickered.

"It waits in the water," she murmured. "It watches."

Elias' fingers tightened on his notebook. "Why Claire? Why now?"

Mrs. Harding let out a shuddering breath. "It's not just her." She finally looked at him, her eyes filled with a terror so raw it made his skin crawl. "There were others before her. Others who—" She stopped. Her breath hitched.

The candle's flame flickered violently.

Then, just as suddenly, it snuffed out.

The room plunged into darkness.

Elias' heart seized. The air turned thick, oppressive, carrying with it a sound so faint he almost didn't notice it.

Dripping.

Slow. Steady.

Coming from the hallway.

Mrs. Harding gasped, her hands flying to her mouth.

Elias turned his head toward the sound, his own breath locked in his chest.

The floorboards creaked.

Something was there.

A shape stood in the hallway, barely visible in the shadows.

Wet. Motionless.

Watching.

Then, the whisper returned, curling around the silence like fingers around a throat.

"She's still in the water."

Elias didn't wait. He grabbed Mrs. Harding's arm and yanked her toward the door.

Behind them, the whispering grew louder.

And then—

The candle reignited on its own.

8

Beneath the Surface

The candle's flame wavered, casting elongated shadows across the walls. Elias barely had time to react before Mrs. Harding gasped, clutching at his arm. Her skin was cold, clammy, her breath shallow and ragged.

The figure in the hallway had not moved. It remained there, its form barely distinguishable from the darkness around it, except for the unmistakable wet sheen on its skin. A drip echoed in the silence—slow, deliberate. The sound of something that had emerged from deep, unholy waters.

Elias' instincts screamed at him to run, but he forced himself to remain still, gripping Mrs. Harding's wrist. The only thing worse than seeing it was turning his back to it.

Then, it stepped forward.

A single, deliberate step.

Elias sucked in a sharp breath as the candle's glow flickered across the figure's face—or what should have been a face. What he saw instead sent a surge of cold terror through his veins.

The skin was pallid, stretched thin like old parchment. Its lips were slightly parted, but no breath came from within. Its eyes... there were no eyes. Only empty sockets filled with something that moved, a swirling darkness that seemed to shift like liquid.

A voice slithered through the air, hollow and waterlogged.

"She never left the river."

Elias yanked Mrs. Harding backward. She was trembling violently, a strangled sob escaping her throat as she clung to his sleeve.

"Claire?" Elias forced the name past his lips. His voice wavered, uncertain.

The thing tilted its head at an unnatural angle, as if considering the word, tasting it. Then, it whispered again—soft, but heavy with something that was neither human nor entirely dead.

"She called for help. But no one listened."

Elias felt his stomach twist. He had heard those words before—whispered at the river, woven into the static of his recorder. Claire's voice. Or something using it.

Mrs. Harding's grip tightened. "It's not her," she choked out. "It wears her face, but it's not her."

Elias swallowed hard, his mind racing. "Then what does it want?"

The candle's flame flickered violently.

"To be remembered."

The room plunged into chaos. The candle sputtered out once more, and in the pitch darkness, something lunged.

Mrs. Harding screamed.

Elias barely had time to react before he was yanked forward, an icy grip locking around his wrist. The cold burned, seeping through his skin like tendrils of freezing water. His body stiffened, every muscle locking in place as a pressure—impossible and suffocating—pressed against his chest.

The whispers surged around him, growing louder, overlapping. Some were Claire's voice, desperate and pleading. Others were low, ancient, indecipherable.

Then, he saw it.

Not just the thing in front of him, but something more. A flickering vision forced into his mind—a memory that did not belong to him.

The river at night. The water black, churning.

A girl struggling beneath the surface. Hands reaching for the shore.

And another pair of hands—pale, bony—grasping her ankles, pulling her down.

Claire's last breath escaping in a desperate, soundless scream.

Elias gasped, the vision shattering as he was thrown backward. His body hit the floor hard, pain jolting through his spine. He scrambled to his feet, his breath coming in ragged gulps.

The figure had vanished.

Mrs. Harding was on her knees, sobbing into her hands.

Elias staggered, his legs unsteady as he reached for her shoulder. "We have to go."

She didn't respond.

"We have to go, now!"

Something shifted in the hallway—a sound like wet fabric peeling from skin.

Elias grabbed Mrs. Harding's arm and pulled her to her feet. This time, she didn't resist. They stumbled toward the door, nearly tripping over themselves in their desperation.

The moment they crossed the threshold, the temperature shifted. The suffocating weight lifted. The air was still.

Elias slammed the door behind them.

They stood in silence, their breath fogging in the cold air.

Mrs. Harding wiped at her face with trembling hands. "It won't stop," she whispered. "It never stops."

Elias looked back at the house. The windows were dark, empty. But he could still hear it.

The dripping.

Somewhere inside, the whisper came again—soft, but unyielding.

"Come back to the water."

9

The Drowned Shall Rise

The night was thick with an unnatural stillness. Elias and Mrs. Harding stood outside the house, their breath forming pale ghosts in the cold air. The weight of what had just happened pressed against Elias' chest like a vice, but there was no time to dwell on it. He needed answers, and he needed them fast.

"We can't stay here," he said, his voice hoarse. "It knows we see it."

Mrs. Harding gave a weak nod, but her hands were still shaking, her lips slightly parted as though she wanted to say something—something terrible—but couldn't force the words out.

Elias turned toward the road, scanning the empty streets. A dense fog had begun to creep through the town, rolling in thick tendrils that slithered along the pavement. It felt alive, like fingers reaching out, searching.

They needed to move.

"Come on," he urged, taking Mrs. Harding by the arm and pulling her along.

Every step felt like they were wading deeper into something unseen, something waiting. The town felt abandoned now, as if every house, every shadow, was watching.

They made it to Elias' car, and he fumbled with the keys, his hands unsteady. The moment he unlocked the door, Mrs. Harding practically collapsed into the passenger seat. Elias slid in behind the wheel, starting the engine.

But before he could shift into drive, something flickered in the rearview mirror.

A shape.

Elias froze, his blood turning to ice.

At first, it was nothing—just darkness shifting within the fog. But then, the shape solidified.

A figure stood at the edge of the mist, barely visible under the flickering streetlight.

Claire.

She was standing barefoot on the cracked pavement, her white baptismal dress clinging to her body as though still soaked with water. Her head tilted slightly, strands of wet hair plastered against her pale face.

Elias' fingers clenched around the steering wheel.

Mrs. Harding turned slowly, following his gaze. The moment she saw the figure, she let out a choked sob.

"No," she whispered. "No, it's not her."

Elias knew she was right.

The Claire in the rearview mirror didn't move like a person. She twitched, her limbs almost too stiff, her feet hovering just above the pavement as if gravity had no claim over her.

And then, ever so slowly, she smiled.

It was the wrong kind of smile.

A knowing, hollow, impossibly wide grin that stretched across her face like something wearing a mask of human skin.

Elias' breath caught in his throat.

Then—

She moved.

Not walked. Not ran.

But *shifted*.

One moment, she was at the edge of the mist. The next, she was closer—impossibly close. Inches from the trunk of the car, her empty eyes staring straight into Elias through the mirror.

A single droplet of water rolled down the glass.

Elias slammed his foot on the gas.

The tires screeched against the pavement as the car lurched forward. Mrs. Harding let out a gasp, gripping the dashboard as they sped down the fog-choked road.

Elias' heart pounded. He refused to look back. He couldn't.

But the whisper still came.

Inside the car.

From behind them.

"You can't run from the water."

Mrs. Harding screamed.

Elias swerved, nearly losing control of the car. His breath was ragged, his mind racing. He reached for the rearview mirror—

And froze.

Claire was gone.

Only the fog remained, curling hungrily along the road behind them.

Elias drove without stopping, without speaking. He didn't dare slow down, not until the last remnants of the fog were swallowed by the darkness behind them.

Not until he was sure they were alone.

But even then, he could still hear it.

The slow, steady sound of dripping water.

10

The Water Remembers

The road stretched out endlessly ahead, swallowed by darkness on either side. The car's headlights cut through the mist, but the fog still clung to the pavement, thick and restless. Elias gripped the wheel tightly, his knuckles white as he struggled to keep his hands steady. Mrs. Harding sat beside him, her breathing shallow, her face streaked with tears.

Neither of them spoke.

The silence in the car was deafening, but Elias wasn't sure if he wanted to break it. His mind raced with the image of Claire—*or whatever that thing was*—standing on the road, her dress dripping, her smile stretched too wide, her voice slithering through the air.

"You can't run from the water."

The words wouldn't leave him. They burrowed deep, looping over and over like a broken record.

Elias' throat was dry. His pulse hammered in his ears. He forced himself to focus on the road, though his mind kept drifting back to the river—to the way Claire's voice had echoed in the recording, to the moment she had vanished beneath the surface, swallowed whole.

Mrs. Harding shifted beside him, wrapping her arms around herself. She looked smaller, frailer, as if the encounter had drained whatever strength she had left.

"We need to go to the church," she murmured finally, her voice barely above a whisper.

Elias flicked his eyes toward her. "What?"

She turned, meeting his gaze. "We need to go to the church," she repeated, her voice steadier this time. "It's the only place left."

Elias hesitated. His instinct was to keep driving, to put as much distance as possible between them and whatever had taken Claire. But something about Mrs. Harding's tone made his stomach tighten.

He knew fear when he heard it.

"What's at the church?" he asked, his voice hoarse.

She swallowed hard. "Answers."

The word sent a shiver through him.

Elias exhaled sharply and tightened his grip on the wheel. He didn't like it. Every rational part of him screamed that they should keep going—leave this cursed town behind, never look back.

But he also knew that running wouldn't change anything.

Whatever was happening, it wasn't finished with them.

With a slow nod, he turned the wheel, guiding the car toward the narrow road that led to St. Benedict's Church.

The fog thickened as they drove, swallowing the trees on either side, making it impossible to see more than a few feet ahead. The air in the car grew colder, and Elias caught himself shivering despite the heat blasting through the vents.

He cast a quick glance at the rearview mirror.

The backseat was empty.

But the feeling was still there.

A presence.

Watching.

Waiting.

Mrs. Harding sucked in a sharp breath.

Elias turned just in time to see the shadow loom in front of them.

His instincts took over. He slammed on the brakes, the tires screeching against the pavement as the car skidded violently to a stop. The force threw them forward, the seatbelt biting into Elias' shoulder.

For a moment, everything was still.

The fog curled around the car like grasping fingers.

Then—

A slow, deliberate knock on the driver's side window.

Elias' blood ran cold.

He turned his head, dread clawing its way up his spine.

A figure stood just beyond the glass.

Not Claire.

Not human.

Its face was obscured by the fog, but Elias could see the shape of it—thin, almost stretched. The fingers that pressed against the window were long, too long, the nails blackened and chipped.

Another knock.

This time, louder.

Elias' breath came in shallow gasps. His mind screamed at him to move, to drive, to do anything but sit there frozen.

Then the figure bent down.

And whispered through the glass.

"The water remembers."

The voice was neither male nor female, neither old nor young. It was something else entirely.

Something ancient.

Something that did not belong in this world.

The temperature in the car plummeted. Frost spiderwebbed across the windshield. Mrs. Harding let out a strangled sob, pressing herself against the passenger door.

Elias reached for the gearshift with a shaking hand.

The figure's lips stretched into a grotesque grin.

Then—

It vanished.

Gone.

Like it had never been there at all.

The fog shifted, thinning slightly. The road ahead cleared.

Elias didn't waste a second.

He slammed his foot on the gas.

The car lurched forward, the engine roaring as they sped down the road, away from whatever had just been standing outside.

But even as the church came into view, standing like a dark silhouette against the night sky, one thought consumed Elias completely.

"The water remembers."

And it was waiting for him.

11

The Whispering Font

The iron gates of St. Benedict's stood ajar, creaking softly as the wind slithered through them. The church loomed ahead, its stone walls bathed in the dim glow of the streetlights. The stained-glass windows were dark, lifeless, as if the very soul of the building had been drained away.

Elias pulled the car to a stop in the gravel lot. For a moment, neither he nor Mrs. Harding moved. The air was thick, charged with something unseen, something that made the hairs on the back of Elias' neck stand on end.

Mrs. Harding clutched her cross necklace so tightly her knuckles turned white. "I don't want to go in there," she whispered.

Elias swallowed hard, his pulse hammering in his ears. "We don't have a choice."

A single bell tolled from the steeple, though the church hadn't rung its bells in years. The sound sent a chill through Elias, as if something was watching from above, waiting.

He stepped out of the car, gravel crunching beneath his boots. Mrs. Harding followed hesitantly, casting nervous glances toward the darkened windows. The front doors were shut, heavy oak with iron handles, but as Elias reached for them, they creaked open on their own.

The inside of the church was cold. Unnaturally cold.

Candles flickered along the walls, their flames too still, too quiet. The pews stretched out in neat rows, untouched by time, but the air smelled wrong—damp, like old wood that had soaked in river water.

Elias' breath came out in shallow puffs.

Something was whispering.

Not aloud. Not in the air.

But in his head.

He turned to Mrs. Harding. She was trembling, eyes darting around the vast nave of the church. "Do you hear that?" she asked, voice barely audible.

Elias nodded.

The whispers were coming from the front.

From the baptismal font.

He forced himself to move forward, each step slow, deliberate. The stone basin stood in the center of the altar, filled to the brim with dark water. It shouldn't have been there—St. Benedict's had been dry for years. The old priest had drained the font when the congregation dwindled.

And yet, the water rippled.

Elias could feel it pulsing, as if something beneath the surface was breathing.

Mrs. Harding clutched his arm. "Elias," she rasped, pointing at the water.

A face was forming beneath the surface.

Claire's face.

Her eyes were wide, her lips parted as if she were screaming, though no sound came. Her hair floated around her in dark tendrils, and her hands pressed against the inside of the water, as though she were trapped behind glass.

Elias took an involuntary step back.

The whispers grew louder.

"*It's not her,*" Mrs. Harding choked out. "It wants you to think it is, but it's not her."

Claire's mouth moved beneath the water, but the words were distorted, warped. The surface rippled violently, and Elias felt it then—*the pull.*

His feet inched forward against his will.

The water wanted him.

Needed him.

Mrs. Harding yanked him back, her grip surprisingly strong. "We have to go," she hissed.

But Elias couldn't move.

The water began to rise.

Slowly at first, then faster, spilling over the edges of the font, sliding across the marble floor in unnatural patterns. It wasn't just water. It was *alive*.

It slithered toward them, reaching with grasping tendrils.

Mrs. Harding gasped as the first tendril wrapped around her ankle, ice-cold and pulsing. She kicked frantically, her foot slipping on the wet stone.

Elias grabbed her, pulling her away just as another tendril lunged for him. The whispers turned to screams, voices rising in a deafening chorus.

"You can't run from the water."

The candles flickered wildly, the flames bending toward the font as if drawn by some unseen force. The water surged forward, a wave of darkness rushing toward them.

Elias turned and ran.

Mrs. Harding stumbled beside him, her breath coming in short gasps. The water chased them, sloshing over the floor with unnatural speed. The church doors loomed ahead—still open.

But something was waiting.

A figure stood in the doorway.

Claire.

Or what used to be Claire.

Her eyes were hollow, her skin gray and waterlogged. Her dress clung to her body, still dripping, though no water fell to the floor.

She raised one hand, palm outward.

"Stay," she whispered.

The water surged behind them.

Elias had no choice.

He grabbed Mrs. Harding and dove.

Straight through Claire.

Through the doors.
Through the cold night air—
And into the silence beyond.

12

Drenched in Shadows

Elias hit the ground hard, the breath knocked from his lungs as he tumbled onto the damp grass outside the church. The cold night air bit into his skin, but he barely registered it. His mind was still reeling, his pulse hammering like a drum.

Beside him, Mrs. Harding groaned, struggling to push herself up. Her hands trembled violently, her nails caked with mud. She turned her wide, terrified eyes toward the church.

The doors were still open.

But Claire was gone.

The interior of St. Benedict's had changed. No longer did the flickering candlelight illuminate the pews. No longer did the baptismal font stand at the altar. The church was swallowed in darkness—so deep and absolute that it looked more like a gaping maw than a place of worship.

The whispers had stopped.

Only silence remained.

Elias pushed himself onto his elbows, his head swimming. Every instinct screamed at him to run, to put as much distance between himself and the church as possible. But something rooted him to the spot.

He wasn't sure if it was fear.

Or something else.

Mrs. Harding grabbed his arm, her nails digging into his skin. "We can't stay here," she choked out. "We have to leave. Now."

Elias turned his gaze to her, but before he could respond, a new sound broke the stillness.

A slow, deliberate dripping.

His stomach twisted.

Drip.

Drip.

Drip.

He followed the sound with his eyes, dread tightening like a noose around his throat. The roof of the church was leaking. Water trickled down from the edges, sliding down the stone walls, pooling at the threshold.

But the sky was clear.

Not a single cloud.

The stars shimmered above, untouched by storm or rain.

And yet, the church bled water.

Mrs. Harding must have noticed it too because she sucked in a sharp breath, her grip tightening on Elias' arm.

Then—

A single wet footprint appeared on the ground before them.

Then another.

And another.

Leading away from the church.

Leading toward them.

Elias scrambled back, dragging Mrs. Harding with him. His heart slammed against his ribs as the footprints grew closer, the wet earth squelching under invisible weight.

Then the night air shifted.

A breath.

Right behind him.

Slow. Cold.

Elias didn't turn. He couldn't.

A hand brushed the back of his neck—clammy, too light, barely there.

Mrs. Harding let out a strangled gasp.

That was all it took.

Elias lunged forward, grabbing her wrist, yanking her toward the car. The gravel crunched beneath his feet as he sprinted, his lungs burning, his body screaming for him to move faster.

Behind him, the whispering returned.

But this time, it wasn't inside his head.

It was everywhere.

Swirling through the trees, wrapping around his limbs, seeping into his bones.

"The water remembers."

The words crashed over him like a wave, nearly knocking him off balance.

The car was just ahead.

A few more steps.

Mrs. Harding reached the passenger door first, fumbling with the handle. "Hurry!" she cried.

Elias yanked open the driver's side door, throwing himself inside. His hands were slick with sweat as he jammed the keys into the ignition, twisting violently.

The engine sputtered.

Coughed.

Then died.

"No, no, no," Elias hissed, his shaking fingers twisting the key again.

The whispers grew louder.

Closer.

The air in the car turned damp, thick with the scent of river water.

Mrs. Harding was sobbing, her hands gripping the dashboard. "Elias," she whimpered.

His gaze shot to the rearview mirror.

And his stomach dropped.

The backseat was filled with water.

It sloshed against the seats, dark and endless, stretching into a void that should not have existed within the car. And floating in the middle of it—

Claire.

Her hair fanned out, her eyes open, locked onto his. Her lips parted, mouthing something silent and desperate.

The doors slammed shut on their own.

The car filled with the sound of rushing water.

Elias barely had time to gasp before the first icy tendril wrapped around his throat.